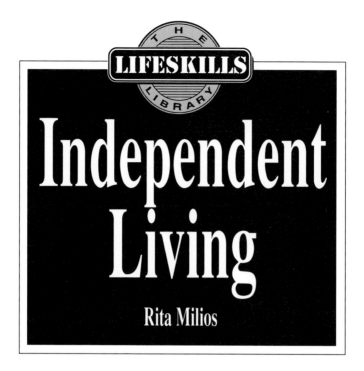

Independent Living

Rita Milios

THE ROSEN PUBLISHING GROUP, INC.

NEW YORK

Published in 1992 by The Rosen Publishing Group, Inc.
29 East 21st Street, New York, 10010

First Edition
Copyright 1992 by The Rosen Publishing Group, Inc.

Manufactured in the United States of America

Library of Congress Cataloging-in-Publication Data
Milios, Rita.
      Independent living / by Rita Milios
            p.   cm. — (The Lifeskills library)
      Includes bibliographical references and index.
      Summary: Discusses the pros and cons of living on your own, including where to live, finances, and the realities of living alone.
      ISBN 0-8239-1454-2
      1. Youth—United States—Life skills guides—Juvenile literature. 2. Life skills—United States—Juvenile literature. 3. Living alone—United States—Juvenile literature. [1. Life skills. 2. Living alone.] I. Title II. Series: Life skills library.
HQ796.M479 1992   92-24422
640—dc20   CIP
                                                                        AC

CONTENTS

WHAT IS INDEPENDENT LIVING?

A re you living away from your family? Are you on your own? Are you taking care of yourself? If you are, you are living independently.

Independent living means that you alone are responsible for your daily life. You may live alone, or with others. You may rent a room, an apartment, or a house. But you pay for your own place. You pay for your food and clothing. You pay for other expenses. You alone make many of the decisions that affect your life.

If you are a teen reading this book, you may already be living independently. Or you may just be thinking about it. But sooner or later you will be on

---

Living on your own means taking responsibility for all household chores.

your own. This book is for, and about, that time. It will help you when you are on your own. It will help you *get ready* to be on your own.

Being responsible for yourself is not easy. It means giving up the luxury of having things done for you. No one cooks your meals. No one cleans your home. No one reminds you of appointments. No one helps you with everyday problems.

Being responsible for yourself means making your own decisions. It means planning your own routine. It means depending on yourself. It may mean being alone for the first time in your life.

Before You Live on Your Own

Before you can seriously begin to think about living independently, you must have a secure source of income.

Any landlord from whom you wish to rent will want to know how you are going to pay each month. He or she will want references who can prove that your income is sufficient. You may also be required to give information about your bank checking or saving account.

Some landlords will not rent to minors. Others require a guardian or parent to cosign the lease.

If you have a full-time job, it must pay enough to support you. If you are in school, you must show that you have a scholarship that will support you, or a parent or guardian who will guarantee to pay for your expenses.

Guidelines set up by the U.S. government say that a person's rent should not be greater than 30 percent of his or her gross income. Some landlords require applicants to meet this standard.

So you see that living independently requires a lot more of you than just wanting to be on your own.

Some Questions to Be Answered

If you are thinking about living independently—now or in the future—you may have many questions. How do you find a place to live? How do you take care of a home? What about legal issues, like signing a rental agreement? How do you take care of yourself and stay healthy?

All of these questions and more will be answered in the pages ahead. Let's get started by looking at your personal finances.

INDEPENDENT FINANCES

Living on your own usually means paying for everything yourself. You must see that you have enough money each month to pay your rent. You must have money for food, clothes, utilities, and school expenses. You should set aside money each month for these *fixed expenses*. It's a good idea to make a *budget*, a written plan of how you will spend your money.

In addition to making a budget, you should learn to use the services of a bank. A bank gives you a safe place to keep your money. You can also earn extra money—*interest*—on the money the bank holds for you. You should have both a *checking account* and a *savings account*.

It is important to keep good records of your income and your spending.

Checking Account

A checking account allows you to keep your money in a safe place—the bank. When you pay bills, instead of using cash you write a check. Checks are promises that the people to whom they are written can get their money from your bank. The bank takes the amount of the check from your account. Always be sure that you have enough money in your account to cover, or pay for, the checks that you write.

It is very important to keep good records of the money you put into and take out of your checking account. Your checkbook has a section for keeping these records. Be sure to enter the amount of each check that you write. Then subtract that amount from your previous total. This is your *balance*, or the amount that you have left.

Before opening a checking account, ask several banks about the services they offer. Some banks allow you to write as many checks as you want without a charge. This is called "no service fee" checking. To get it, you have to keep a large balance in the bank in either your checking or your savings account, or both. Otherwise you have to pay a small *service fee* each month.

Savings Account

When you save at a bank, you have a *savings account*. This account earns *interest* each month.

For saving your money in an account, the bank will give you interest, an additional amount of money. The amount is based on a percentage of the amount you have in the account. Check at your local bank for the savings plans that are available. You may want a regular savings account that pays a small fixed percentage in interest each month. In this account you can withdraw your money at any time. You may want a special savings program that pays higher interest. In such a plan you have to leave your money in the bank for a certain length of time. If you take it out early, you lose the interest.

Credit Cards

Credit cards are used in place of money to make purchases. When you use a credit card, you actually borrow time to pay for your purchase. The company that gave you the card then bills you for the money. If you pay it back later than within a month, the credit card company will charge you interest. This interest is usually much higher than the interest you earn on savings.

Credit cards may seem like an easy way to pay for your purchases. But people often get into trouble using them. They buy more than they can pay for each month. Charging can lead to financial disaster. It is wiser to save for items that you want.

Independent living means you must begin to think smarter financially. You must become an aware consumer. You must learn to live within a budget.

CHAPTER 3

WHERE WILL YOU LIVE?

You have made up your mind to live independently. Now you must find a place to live. How will you decide what type of living space is right for you? Will you rent an apartment? A room? Something else?

First you should think about *where* that space should be. You want to live in a location that is near the places you go to frequently, like school, work, or your family's home. Other things must be considered about the location.

Is your living space close to a grocery store, drugstore, or other places where you shop? Is it close to friends' homes? Relatives' homes?

Is transportation available? If you use a bus to get to school or work, is the bus stop nearby? How

---

Your local newspaper is one of the best resources for hunting down apartments.

often does the bus run? Can you get where you need to go using just one bus? Or do you have to transfer?

Is the neighborhood safe? Would you feel safe walking alone there at night? Do you think your valuables would be safe when you were away?

What kind of neighbors would you have? What ages are they? You probably would not feel at home in a community of senior citizens. You might prefer a "singles" location. Or you might like a community that includes parents and children.

After thinking about these things, you are ready to think about the *kind* of place you want.

Housing Options

When you think of living alone, you probably think of an apartment. But there are other options that can be less expensive.

Room rentals are an option. Many times you can rent a room in a house or apartment that is owned by another person. This is probably less expensive. You pay only for a bedroom and the use of a bathroom (which may be down the hall). You may be allowed space in the owner's refrigerator to store food. You might not be allowed to use the stove.

Efficiency apartments are another option. These usually include a bathroom and a kitchen area. They may have a separate entrance. Efficiency apartments may be in an apartment building or a separate section of a private home.

Questions to Ask

Whether you are thinking of renting a room, an efficiency apartment, or a regular apartment, ask yourself these questions:

• Is the place *furnished* or *unfurnished*? Rooms usually come furnished. Some apartments come complete with everything: furniture, appliances, dishes, and often even linens and towels.

But furnished apartments cost more money. If you are short of money, you can save by renting a room or an unfurnished apartment. You will have to bring your own furniture, linens, and dishes. (Unfurnished apartments usually come with a refrigerator and a stove.)

• What can you afford? When you first start to live independently, you may need to start small. You can probably get by for the least money if you rent a single room.

• Does the place have enough security? Is the entrance well lighted? Would you have a separate key? If you would live in a building with others, is there a common door that everyone uses? Is it always locked? Is there a speaker for announcing visitors?

• Is there parking space for your car or bicycle?

• Where are the laundry facilities?

• Are there two exits in case of fire? Is there a smoke alarm in your apartment?

• Is there enough light in the hallways and on the stairs?

FINDING YOUR
DREAM PLACE

You have thought about your needs. You have thought about what you can afford. You are ready to look for a place that is right for you. What do you do first?

Start by looking at advertisements. The *classified ads* in your local paper are a good place to start. Also look for notices posted on bulletin boards in libraries, schools, and stores. Jot down phone numbers and details.

When you call, have a list of questions ready to ask: How much is the rent? What size is the apartment? Is it furnished? Are kitchen appliances provided? Are pets allowed?

Also be prepared to answer the questions the landlord is likely to ask about: your job or other

Asking friends to help is a good way to keep moving expenses under control.

source of income, your bank and personal references, and your reason for moving.

You can also rent through a rental agency or real estate office. Most cities have companies that help people find places to live. The cost of this service is usually paid by the owner, not the renter. Look for ads in the local newspaper or in the Yellow Pages of the telephone book.

At the Appointment

When you go to see a place, keep in mind the items to look for listed in Chapter 3. It is probably a good idea to make a checklist. Check off each item that you are looking for and write any thoughts you may have. If you depend solely on your memory, you may get confused after seeing only a few places.

Finally, before you sign a rental agreement, you might want to check the location. If you don't have a car, take a bus ride from the place to your school or work. Visit the nearest grocery store. Talk with the neighbors. Renting a place is a big step. It will be easier if you think things through carefully and make informed decisions.

A Rental Agreement

Let's say that you have found a place that you want. It is in a good location. It is affordable. It has everything that you need. Now you are ready to sign a *rental agreement* or *lease*. What can you expect?

Following is a typical rental agreement. Read the agreement and the explanations. It is a good idea to have another responsible adult read it also. Remember, a lease is a legal document. Once you sign it, you are legally bound to follow its terms.

The lease first states that it is a legal agreement between two people made on a certain date. You are the *lessee*. The landlord is the *lessor*.

Look now at the circled numbers on the lease.

1. This states the amount of the rent and the part of the utility bill that the lessee must pay. (If you were renting a separate apartment, you would pay the whole utility bill for the apartment.)

2. A security deposit must be paid. When you move out of the rental place, the deposit will be returned to you unless you have damaged the place beyond normal wear and tear.

If you do not live in the rental space for the entire month during the first or last month, you do not have to pay the whole month's utility bill. But while you rent, you must pay the full cost of the utilities even when you are away.

You may not *sublet*—rent your place to someone else—unless the owner agrees.

You may not change the apartment—paint, move major appliances, nail or screw things into the walls or floor—without the permission of the owner. You may not make improvements such as tearing down walls without permission from the owner.

3. The owner is responsible for "major" maintenance such as the repair of appliances and plumbing.

Sample Rental Agreement

This agreement has been entered into on _____, by and between _____, hereinafter called LESSEE and _____, hereinafter called LESSOR.

In consideration of a monthly rent of _____ plus _____% of the utilities ❶ (specifically for gas, electricity, water, trash collection, and basic telephone service) the LESSEE shall be entitled to share, on a month-to-month basis, the residence located at
_____.

The following are mutually agreed upon points:

1. LESSEE will begin tenancy on _____.
2. Rent will be due on the _____ day of each month.
3. The LESSEE shall pay the first and last month's rent in advance before occupying the premises.

❷ 4. The LESSEE shall pay a damage deposit of $_____ before occupying the premises. Within 30 days after departure, if all obligations have been paid in full, and if the premises have been maintained in satisfactory condition, the deposit with any interest required by law, shall be returned to the LESSEE. Any deductions will be itemized in writing and sent to the LESSEE.

5. The initial utility bill and the last month's utility bill will be prorated to coincide with the number of days the LESSEE has agreed to occupy the house (i.e., until the last day of the rental period for that month). Otherwise, no matter how many days the LESSEE is away from the house during the course of a month, the LESSEE is responsible for _____% of the utilities.

6. LESSEE's guests may stay overnight on the premises up to one week.

7. LESSEE shall not sublet the premises without the express consent of the LESSOR.

8. LESSEE shall make no alterations, additions, or improvements to the premises without the express consent of the LESSOR.

(Continued next page)

20

❸ 9. LESSOR shall assume expenses for the major maintenance, cleaning, and repair of the furnace, roof, water heater, central air conditioning, gutters and outside plumbing, and repairs to equipment and major appliances when required in the course of their normal and proper usage.

10. LESSEE shall be responsible for any loss or damage caused by his or her negligence, shall keep plumbing fixtures as clean and safe as condition permits, and shall unstop and keep clear all waste pipes which are for his or her exclusive use.

❹ 11. LESSOR shall not be liable to LESSEE for any damage or injury to the LESSEE nor to the LESSEE's guests, nor for any personal property which is stolen or damaged due to flooding, leaks, fire, malfunction of equipment, structural problems, or for any reason whatever, unless LESSOR's willful negligence can be proved. All persons and personal property in or on said property associated with the LESSEE shall be at the sole risk and responsibility of the LESSEE.

❺ 12. This agreement and the tenancy hereby granted may be terminated at any time by either party hereto by giving to the other party not less than thirty (30) days prior notice in writing. Terminations initiated by the LESSEE must end on the last day of the month.

❻ Special Provisions:

   Both parties have read this agreement, agree to its terms, and each has a copy.

_____   _____
       LESSEE   LESSOR

_____

From *Living with Tenants*, McGraw-Hill, New York, 1986.
Used with permission of the author, Doreen Bierbrier.

You must take everyday care of the appliances, plumbing, and other fixtures.

4.   If you are hurt while you live in the place, the owner is not responsible (except where the law says differently). The owner is not responsible for damage by flood or other disaster.

5.   Either you or the owner can end your agreement by giving at least 30 days' *written* notice.

6.   "Special Provisions" are any additions you and the owner agree on. You might have the right to keep a pet. The owner might agree to paint the premises after a certain period of time.

When you have agreed on the terms, you both sign the agreement. You are now a renter.

Moving In

Once you rent a place, you must take care of a few details before you can move in. You need to:

• Call the gas company, the electric company, and the phone company. Ask to have services started. Allow at least a week for this to be done.

• Call on friends, family, or a moving company to help you on moving day. If you need to rent a truck, call a week or more in advance.

• Pack your belongings in advance. Collect cartons from stores and pack your things carefully. Wrap breakables in plenty of paper. Write on the closed cartons what is packed inside.

• Be as ready as possible on the great day. Try to spend moving day *moving*, not packing.

CHAPTER 5

FURNISHING YOUR PLACE

When you move into your place, you will need furniture, appliances, and other items. Your budget may be small. How can you get everything you need and create a comfortable home at the lowest possible cost?

Furnishing Your Place

It usually costs less to rent an unfurnished apartment. But then you have to furnish it yourself. This costs more money at first. But you pay lower monthly rent over a longer time.

Remember, your first apartment does not have to be a "showcase." If you are creative, you can furnish and decorate with less money. Develop a style of your own. Find items that suit your personality.

Spending a little extra time shopping can help you find just the right item at the right price.

Don't always shop at furniture or department stores. Look for bargains. Try the Salvation Army or other secondhand stores. Also, ask friends or relatives if they have furniture and other items they don't want or that they plan to get rid of. Used furniture is a good way to get started. You can try out decorating ideas inexpensively. If you decide that the "country look" is not for you, for example, you can afford to change to another style later.

Kitchen Items

The kitchen in your new place will probably need the most attention. It needs to be in order as soon as possible so that you can begin eating at home. Eating well at restaurants is too expensive.

Furnish your kitchen with basic needs first. All you really need is a stove, a refrigerator, some dishes, silverware, glasses, and pots and pans. The fancy coffee maker, electric can opener, and food processor can wait.

Plan to stock some staples and a few days' worth of food as soon as you move. You may want to stay in the first few days and work on organizing your place. Take milk, eggs, bread, fruit, and cold cuts with you. You might also take coffee, sugar, tea, breakfast cereal, and snacks.

Garage or tag sales often feature good used furnishings at reasonable prices.

Linens and Bath Items

Be sure to pack linens where you can find them easily on your first night. You will need sheets, pillowcases, towels, and washcloths. You will need at least two sets of sheets and pillowcases (one to sleep on and one to wash). You will need enough towels and washcloths to last from one washing to another—probably six to eight sets. You will need blankets and a comforter or bedspread for your bed.

Household Products

You will have to do your own cleaning in your new place. The following items should get you started:
• If you have carpeting, you may need a portable vacuum cleaner or "electric broom."
• A sponge mop or a wet mop. Sponge mops are easier to use. You can buy one that squeezes the water out with the press of a handle. But you have to buy replacement mop heads every few months.
• A toilet brush.
• Sponges and cloths to wipe off counters, dust furniture, and clean fixtures and appliances.
• Cleaners for floors, greasy appliances, windows, mirrors, and counter tops; scouring powder, furniture polish or oil, and wax or no-wax sealer for kitchen and bathroom floors; and dish-washing soap and bath soap.
• Rubber gloves to protect your hands.
Now you are ready to set up housekeeping.

TAKING CARE OF
YOUR PLACE

If this is your first place, you might not know much about cleaning. This chapter contains suggestions for how and when to do cleaning jobs.

First, think about basic cleaning safety. Cleaning products are chemical solutions. Care must be taken to use them properly and dispose of them properly. Keep the following points in mind:

• Protect yourself from *caustic* products that can burn your eyes or skin. Wear rubber gloves and goggles or safety glasses when using them. Some caustic products are oven cleaners, toilet bowl cleaners, and drain openers.

• Protect yourself and others from poisonous products. Store household products out of reach of young children, who might taste or swallow them.

- Avoid toxic fumes. Fumes from oven cleaners, paint products, and thinners can cause nerve damage. Use these products only with windows open.
- Never smoke when using household products. Some products are *flammable*. They burst into fire easily.
- Rinse cans and bottles and take to a recycling center, if possible. (Most glass, aluminum, and plastics are recyclable.) If throwing away the remainder of a product, pour it down the sink or toilet *only* if it is safe to do so. Read the label.
- Dispose of motor oil, paint thinner, and solvents at an auto service center. They have ways to dispose of them safely.

Big Cleaning Jobs

With luck, housework will not be a big part of your life. But it needs to be done. If you do a little housework every day, it will take less time.

But there will be times when you have to do a major clean-up, perhaps once or twice a year. Here are some of the big jobs you may need to do, and ways to make them easier.

Cleaning Walls. Especially in the kitchen, walls get dirty from dust and grease. You will want to wash them once in a while. Even if you plan to paint, walls should be cleaned. You will not get a good paint job over dirty walls.

Before you put belongings away, check out closets to see if
they need cleaning or painting.

To wash walls, put one cup of ammonia, one cup of vinegar, and one-fourth of a cup of baking soda into one gallon of warm water. Wear rubber gloves. Start at the top of the wall and wash with a sponge. Change the solution as it gets dirty.

Counters and Cupboards. Use the same cleaning solution for counters and cupboards. Start with the highest cupboards. Wipe them clean and let them dry. Then line the bottoms with shelf paper in a pattern that pleases you.

Sinks and Tubs. Scrub enamel kitchen and bathroom sinks, bathtubs, and toilet bowls with scouring powder. If a sink is made of fiberglass or stainless steel, use a nonabrasive cleanser made for the purpose. You can restore the shine on stainless steel by rubbing it with a cloth dipped in baby oil.

Refrigerator. Clean the refrigerator when you first move in. Remove the drawers and shelves and wash them with mild, soapy water. Rinse. Use the same solution to wipe down the inside of the refrigerator and the door shelves. Rinse well and dry.

If the freezer compartment is frozen over or dirty, you will have to defrost it. Unplug the refrigerator. Place a large bowl or tray on the top shelf of the refrigerator. Wait until the ice melts. As it melts, sop up the water with towels. Wash the freezer with soapy water, rinse, and dry. Replace the electric plug.

Oven. Cleaning the oven can be a dirty job. You will need to do it less often if you wipe up spills

When using cleaners, always follow directions. Rubber gloves will protect your skin from harsh chemicals.

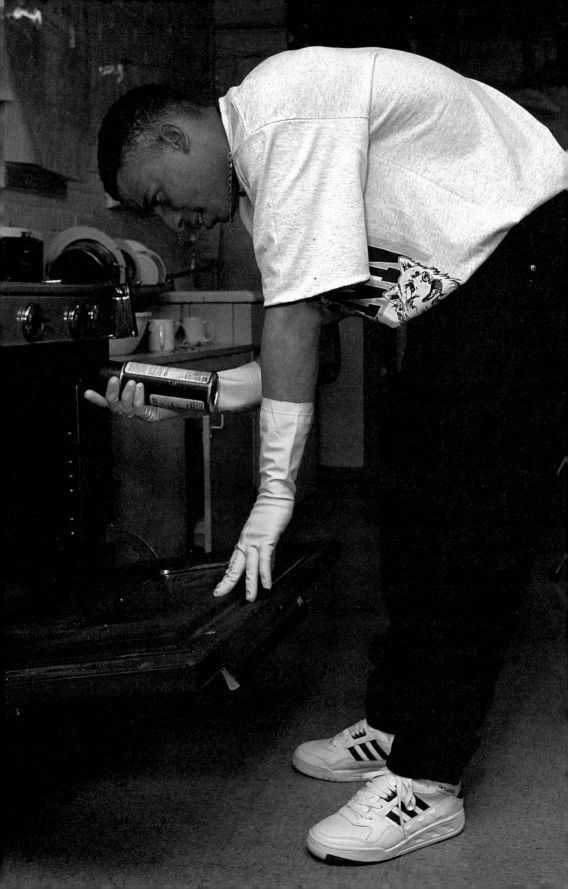

soon after they happen. But if they are already there, here's how to get rid of them.

Sprinkle spills with automatic dishwasher detergent. Cover them with wet paper towels. Wait a few hours, then wipe the spills and detergent away.

Kitchen Floor. If your floor is made of linoleum, vinyl, or no-wax material, clean it with one of the special cleansers made for such floors. A sponge mop works well with these products.

If the floor is very dirty, you may need to clean off a build-up of dirt. Scrub the floor with about half a cup of ammonia in a gallon of water. Use rubber gloves. You may have to scrub with a sponge and scouring pad to clean really dirty areas.

Cleaning the Bathroom. Start by cleaning the shower or tub. If the wall is tiled, you may need to clean the *grout*. This is the material between the tiles that holds them together. Grout sometimes gets mildewed. Mildew is a fungus that makes black stains on the grout.

Several commercial mildew stain removers are available. But you can make your own grout cleaner for less money. Mix three cups of baking soda with one cup of warm water to form a paste. Rub it on the grout with an old toothbrush. Rinse well.

Use scouring powder to scrub the sink and the shower if they are ceramic or tile. Rinse well.

Cleaning the Toilet. You can use scouring powder. It is inexpensive and does a good job. Be sure to use only one cleaner at a time. Mixing products can create toxic fumes.

You can also use liquid chlorine bleach to brighten your toilet. Pour half a cup into the bowl and let it stand for ten minutes. Then clean it with a brush and flush.

Windows, Mirrors, and Glass. You can buy commercial spray cleaners for glass. Or you can make an inexpensive cleaner by mixing two teaspoons of white vinegar with one quart of warm water. Apply with a sponge and dry with a soft cloth. Cut-up old T-shirts work well.

Start with the upper window and work down. Clean the inside with horizontal strokes and the outside with vertical strokes. Then if you have streaks, you can tell which side they are on.

Daily Chores. A neat home is a happier home. To keep your place in order, do a few simple chores each day. Try to get into the habit of "picking up" each day. Here's how:

• Make your bed. Tuck in sheets, straighten blankets, and pull up the comforter or bedspread. Your bed will be ready for you the next time.

• Wash dishes and put them away each day. Pick up your clothes and hang them up. Move items left on tables back where they belong.

• Wipe off counter tops when finished with dishes. Clean sinks regularly to prevent a build-up of soap scum and dirt. Dust surfaces.

• Sweep kitchen floor after dinner. Get rid of dirt and crumbs that could attract bugs.

Now you know how to take care of your new home. Let's look at ways to take better care of *you*.

PLAYING IT SAFE WHEN LIVING ON YOUR OWN

When you live alone, *you* must take care of you. You must be responsible for your own health and safety.

How can you be safe in a place all by yourself? First, you must make it secure. See to it that your place has security locks. Take care that your home is free of dangerous items. Be careful about accidents. Here are some helpful hints for indoor safety:

Safety in the Kitchen

• Prevent falls. Keep a stepladder handy to reach items on high shelves.

• Keep a box of baking soda near the stove. If a fire starts, throw some on the flames.

• Keep a portable fire extinguisher handy.

It is always a good idea to lock your door when you are at home.

Safety in the Bathroom

• Check to see if your bathroom has a *ground fault circuit interrupter* (GFCI) in place. This is a replacement for a standard electric outlet. It shuts off electricity when there is a break, or interruption, in the circuit. If you drop your hair dryer into a sink filled with water, for instance, the electric circuit will be broken, preventing possible electrocution. If your place does not have a GFCI, ask your landlord to install one.

• Tubs should be slip-proof. If your tub is slippery, buy a rubber mat.

• The bathroom is not the best place for medications. Warm, moist air can change the chemicals. Store them in a hall closet or other area.

Safe Hallways and Stairs

• Make sure hallways and stairs have good lighting. Do not use throw rugs near stairways.

General Safety

• Have at least one smoke detector for each floor. Make sure that the batteries are fresh.

• Avoid slippery throw rugs. Tape them down .

Home Security

You should check the safety of the outside of your place too. Here are some things to do to keep it secure:

• Make sure all windows have locks. Use them.

• Put dead bolts on doors. Ordinary locks are too easy to wedge open with a credit card or other small objects.

- Have a phone by your bed for emergency calls.
- Keep a list of emergency numbers by each phone: numbers for the police, fire department, emergency squad, a neighbor, and a relative.
- Do not put your full name on your mailbox, use only your last name.
- If you live in an apartment building with a security front door, never prop it open.
- Never open the security door for someone you don't know. If someone is buzzing the doorbells of all of the apartments, call security.
- Never open your door to a stranger.
- If you go on vacation, place a timer on one or two lights to make it look as if someone is home.
- Ask a trusted neighbor to keep an eye on your place while you are away.

Keep In Touch

It is even more important when you are on your own to know people you can count on. Stay in touch with family and friends. Make an effort to keep old relationships going.

You are the one who has moved. Most of your family and friends still have the same routines. They may forget to call you, so don't wait. Call them. Set up a new schedule to include time with friends and relatives.

Make it a point to meet new people and make new friends. You can never have too many friends or too much support when you are on your own.

TAKING CARE OF YOURSELF BY YOURSELF

Being by yourself means taking care of your own personal needs. You must take responsibility for these needs now.

Health Insurance

Now that you are living alone, you need to keep in mind a number of important aspects of your life that always were a concern of your parents or guardian. Among them is health insurance. If you are still a minor, you are probably covered under your parent's policy. Most health policies cover full-time students until they are 21 years of age; some, 23 or 24. If you are employed, you may get health insurance as a benefit. If not, coverage for yourself should be one of your first concerns.

39

Keeping some of the "basic foods" on hand will help in planning and preparing foods.

Another matter that your parents may have taken care of for you until now is the scheduling and payment of regular medical and dental checkups. If you have a family doctor or dentist, try to keep up with that important responsibility. If not, most cities have medical and dental clinics that charge fees scaled to patients' ability to pay.

Nutrition and Exercise

In your own "castle", there is no longer someone to say "Eat your vegetables. No cookies before dinner." Your eating habits are up to you.

To feel your best you must get proper nutrition. That means eating foods from all of the food groups: bread, grains, and pasta; fruits and vegetables; milk and other dairy products; meats and seafoods; and fats and oils.

Here are some suggestions to help you:

• Eat a good breakfast. Your body has had no food for at least eight hours. It needs fuel to get you through the morning. If you are too hurried to cook, have cereal and fruit with milk, or try an "instant breakfast" drink mixed with milk.

• Get in the habit of fixing yourself a full dinner. Don't let being alone keep you from "taking the trouble." Try new recipes. Make it fun.

• Invite a friend or neighbor over for dinner. Try to set up an exchange with someone else who lives alone to fix dinner for each other once a week.

—

Any meal tastes better when it's shared with a friend.

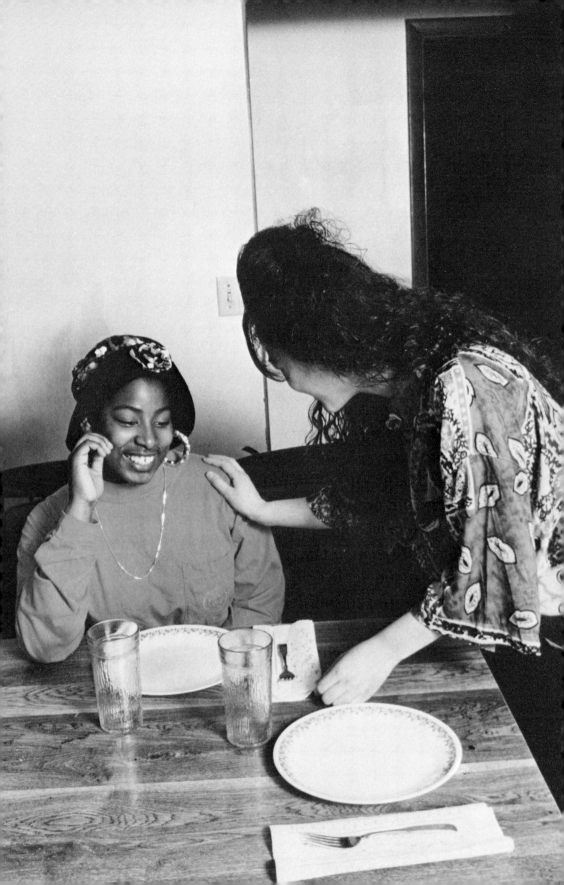

• Choose healthful foods. Think about nutrition as well as convenience. Try to choose fresh foods over processed foods. Be stingy about canned foods, frozen foods, and snacks; they often have too much fat, sugar, or salt (or all three).

To feel your best, you also need to plan regular exercise. Here are some suggestions:

• Go for a walk. Go to a gym. Call a friend to go with you. Exercise at least three times a week.

• Never ride when you can walk. If you only have a few blocks to go, don't drive or take the bus. A daily walk is probably the best (and cheapest) exercise you can do.

• Exercise is movement. Make cleaning time an exercise time. Stretch when you dust. Bend to pick up things on the floor. Keep moving.

Personal Hygiene

Like housekeeping, personal hygiene requires regular daily care. Brushing your teeth, bathing, washing your hair, laundering your clothes, and changing sheets and towels are all necessary to keep you clean and healthy. Besides, when you look your best, you feel better about yourself.

In some ways, living alone makes hygiene easier. There is no line at the bathroom. Its all yours.

Allow yourself more time when you can. Run a large bubble bath. Relax and soak as long as you like. Scrub and trim fingernails and toenails. Condition your hair. Be good to yourself.

Planning Your Time

Make it a point to look past the day you are living. You probably have some long-term goals, such as what you want to do in life. To work towards those goals, you need to set short-term goals to keep you headed in the right direction. Take time to think about what you need to do and want to do in the week ahead. If you are in school, concentrate on your program and making the best possible record. If you have a job, think about ways to do it better and advance toward more responsibility—and pay.

Have a positive attitude. Look for the good in every situation. Decide to be in charge of your own happiness. Try each day to do the following:

• Do something nice for yourself. Do something that you enjoy.

• Do something nice for someone else. Reach out to others. Be kind.

• Do what needs to be done that day. Discipline yourself. Things get done only if you do them. You are in charge. **Just do it!**

• Read. Read for fun. Read to learn. Reading is your door to other people, other places, other ideas.

Living independently can be an exciting and rewarding experience. It can bring you new friends and new relationships. It can help you become more mature. You can become stronger and more sure of yourself. You can take charge of your life. If you plan and work wisely, independent living can offer you a satisfying future.

GLOSSARY
EXPLAINING NEW WORDS

balance The amount of money left in a checking account after all deposits are added and all checks drawn are subtracted.

barter To exchange services for payment or partial payment.

budget Written plan for spending your money.

caustic Capable of burning eyes or skin.

checking account Bank account with which you can write checks up to the amount in your account.

classified ads Advertisements in a special section of the newspaper.

efficiency apartment A living area separate from the rest of a house; a small apartment consisting of a living room, bedroom, kitchen, and bath.

fixed expenses Expenses that must be paid on a regular basis, such as rent and utilities.

flammable Easily set on fire.

ground fault circuit interrupter (GFCI) A circuit breaker that shuts off electrical power if something breaks the circuit.

grout Material that holds ceramic tiles together.

lessee The renter of a rental unit; tenant.

lessor The owner of a rental unit; landlord.

maintenance The care needed to keep a home in good condition.

mildew A fungus that grows in damp, warm places.

rental agreement Written legal obligations of a landlord and a tenant; lease.

savings account Bank account for holding money that earns interest.

security deposit Money from tenant, held by landlord to cover possible property damage. Returned to tenant with interest if property is left in satisfactory condition.

service fee Bank charge for maintaining checking accounts.

sublet To rent all or a portion of a unit that is already being rented.

FOR FURTHER READING

Barrett, Patti. *Too Busy to Clean?* Vermont: Storey Communications, 1990.

Bierbrier, Doreen. *Living with Tenants.* New York: McGraw-Hill, 1986.

Brandwein, Nancy, et al. *The Group House Handbook.* Washington, DC: Acropolis Books, 1982.

Hunter, Linda Mason. *The Healthy Home.* Pennsylvania: Rodale Press, 1989.

Milan, Irene and Mike. *How to Buy and Manage Rental Properties.* New York: Simon & Schuster, 1986.

Reader's Digest. *Household Hints and Handy Tips.* New York: Reader's Digest Association, 1988.

Reader's Digest. *How to Do Just About Anything.* New York: Reader's Digest Association, 1986.

INDEX

About the Author

Rita Milios is author of over a dozen children's books as well as several adult books. Her children's books range from early readers to books for teenagers. Formerly an editor of a children's magazine, Ms. Milios taught writing at Toledo University's Continuing Education Department for seven years. Currently she teaches writing for a national correspondence school.

In addition, Ms. Milios is an educational consultant. She lives in Toledo, Ohio, with her husband and two children.

Photo Credits
All photos on cover and in book by Dru Nadler.
Design & Production by Blackbirch Graphics.